Cambridge Wizard Student Guide

The Curious Incident of the Dog in the Night-time

By Mark Haddon

Richard McRoberts

B.A., M.Ed., M.A.C.E.

CAMBRIDGE
UNIVERSITY PRESS

CAMBRIDGE UNIVERSITY PRESS
Cambridge, New York, Melbourne, Madrid, Cape Town, Singapore, São Paulo

Cambridge University Press
477 Williamstown Road, Port Melbourne, VIC 3207, Australia

www.cambridge.edu.au
Information on this title: www.cambridge.org/9780521613798

© Cambridge University Press 2005

First published 2005
Reprinted 2006, 2007, 2008, 2009

Cover design by Cressaid Media
Cover art by Mark Fox
Typeset by Kath Puxty

Printed in Australia by Ligare Book Printers

Typeface Berkeley System PageMaker® [KP]

National Library of Australia Cataloguing in Publication data

McRoberts, Richard, 1948– .
The curious indicent of the dog in the night-time.
For VCE students
ISBN 978-0-52161-379-8
1. Haddon, Mark. The curious incident of the dog in the night-time.
I. Title. (Series: Cambridge wizard students guide).
823.912

ISBN 13: 9780521613798   paperback

Contents

Notes on the Author   5

Notes on Genre, Structure and Style   7

Background Notes on Mental Disabilities and Illnesses   14

Summary and Commentary   18

Notes on Characters   42

Notes on Themes and Issues   47

What the Critics Say   56

Sample Essays   57

Sample Questions   63

Notes on the Author

Mark Haddon was born in 1964, in Northampton, a town in the midlands of England. His father was an architect, and his mother was a 'home-maker'.

He was 'a depressed and anxious child, with an oversensitivity to everything, an uneasiness in [his] own skin'. Like the fictional Christopher, he was very good at Maths. He read little fiction, preferring instead books on science. However,

> Quote
>
> When I was 13 or 14 I started devouring novels. Literature took quite a while to take me over but it caught up just in time to save me from becoming a mathematician. (Interview quoted in *The Age*, 14 February 2004)

At the age of 16, after having read Tolkien's *Lord of the Rings*, and then Camus' *The Outsider*, he decided he wanted to be a writer.

After completing his B.A. (English) at Oxford, Haddon did a variety of jobs, including working for Community Service Volunteers in Scotland. He was for some time a carer for a patient with multiple sclerosis. In London, he began working for Mencap (the learning disability charity organisation) and the Children's Action Workshop. He has said, of this experience

> Quote
>
> It was full of kids of all ages, with various physical handicaps and learning difficulties, some with mental handicaps. But there were no labels. When you went in there, you had to work out, 'Am I talking to a very articulate seven-year-old, or to a 12-year-old with growth and developmental delay?' That was a real eye-opener. (*The Independent*, 22 January 2004)

He has also known people whose children have Asperger's syndrome, and his nephew has cerebral palsy.

Some years after leaving university, he also began to write and illustrate. He tried his hand at adult fiction, ultimately completing five full-length novels. However, they were never published. He now regards his juvenile efforts as examples of 'over-intellectual 21-year-olds who want to write a big book'. His artistic bent found an outlet in painting and in producing illustrations (cartoons and full colour art), first for magazines and newspapers, and then for children's books. He realised quite soon that he was capable of writing the books as well as illustrating them. *Gilbert's Gobstopper* (1988) and *A Narrow Escape for Princess Sharon* (1989) were the first in what was to be a stream of picture books and juvenile fiction (21 titles by the time he wrote *The Curious Incident*) for kids of varying ages. He says that writing for children taught him not to indulge himself, and to make sure there is a strong story.

In 2003, Haddon wrote a play for the BBC called *Coming Down the Mountain*. It centred on a teenager with Down's syndrome (formerly called Mongolism). Asked if he was particularly interested in mental disabilities, he replied

Quote

'Am I going for the Disability Boxed Set? ... The answer is [No]: [in literature] you always want to get people in extreme situations because it shows who they are. You can't get through a novel on tea parties. You've got to have people in the burning building or the lifeboat. I wanted to be contemporary and ordinary, but have an edge. And this book – Christopher's adventure – does that. (*The Independent*, cited above)

He has pointed out that for many children, life can be every bit as challenging as that of the fictional Christopher (in the novel), with or without a behavioural problem. 'For the more troubled types [of kids in any school] on the edge of the playground, how you get from one day to the next is a mystery'.

The Curious Incident of the Dog in the Night-time was published in mid 2003. It was submitted for the Booker Prize, and immediately generated controversy. The chairman of the judges' panel backed what he called a 'masterly and amazing book', but found himself deserted by the other judges. The novel then picked up the Guardian Children's Fiction prize and the Book Trust teenage fiction award. It hit the bestseller lists and in early 2004 won the prestigeous Whitbread Book of the Year Award. The book has already been translated into 15 languages and published in

32 different countries. Rights to the story have been bought by Warner Brothers, and a film adaptation is being developed.

Haddon lives in Oxford with his wife and two children. He continues to write professionally, as well as teaching part-time (creative writing). A personal note perhaps can be added. In 2003, Haddon's wife 'Sos' (Susan) was cycling near their home. Sos was seven months pregnant. To his horror, she was struck by a speeding Range Rover, and ended up semi-conscious, in a pool of blood, on a country lane. She was airlifted to hospital, where it was discovered that she had a fractured pelvis. Fortunately, she gave birth without complications to their baby son, Zach. Haddon, relieved and grateful, dedicated his Whitbread award to Sos. The book, as you will have noticed, is already dedicated to her.

Notes on Genre, Structure and Style

Genre

The text a 'Rorschach test' for readers

The Curious Incident of the Dog in the Night-time has been described by one review as 'a virtual Rorschach test' of readers' interests and perspectives. [The Rorschach test is the famous inkblot test, where subjects are shown an ambiguous blob-like shape and asked what they think it resembles. Their responses say far more about *their* preoccupations and worries than they do about the inkblot.]

What is it?

What sort of novel is it? A crime story, a social drama, a psychological novel? Is it a comedy, a tragedy or a documentary disguised as fiction? One of the most stimulating aspects of studying the work is the first question of all: what sort of text *is* it?

Psychological drama

The Curious Incident of the Dog in the Night-time mixes several generic traditions. Most obviously, perhaps, it is psychological or personal drama. The gradual unfolding of Christopher's situation – his disability, his relationship with his father and mother, his attempts at grappling with the larger world, his emergent confidence and growth – these are the central preoccupations of the narrative. A superficial reading of the story might suggest that Christopher's predicament is static. But it is only static during the exposition period of the novel. Once his sleuthing leads to his father's wardrobe, a major crisis blows up and things change very rapidly. The motivating factors for the change are (a) his finding out that his father has lied to him, and what's more killed the dog, and (b) discovery that his mother is not dead, but alive and living in London. Christopher's epic (for him) journey in quest of his mother, the reunion, the fallout of that, the return to Swindon, the maths exam, the reconciliation with his father, all these are key passages in what amounts to his transition from helplessness to a kind of semi-autonomy. The novel has been compared to *Catcher in the Rye*, the 1954 bestseller about a troubled adolescent who also runs away, and although the comparison is misleading, the two works do have in common a memorable, 'alienated' protagonist and a dramatic, psychologically compelling story.

Haddon is doing more than just showing us his central character, though, and he uses a clever mix – combining his core genre with other elements. Some are there to add narrative zest to the mix, and all reveal underlying issues.

Murder mystery or 'whodunnit'

Firstly there is the murder mystery or 'whodunnit' dimension. The novel opens with the dead dog, and for more than half the story Christopher devotes considerable energy to trying to find its killer. The mystery is a shrewd device. It is plausible, insofar as a person who loves puzzles and is gifted at deduction would likely try to solve such a mystery. It is engaging, because – like Christopher – *we* want to know what really happened. Most importantly though, the sleuthing leads to discoveries which are themselves keys to the human drama which is going on beyond Christopher's comprehension. The dead dog turns out to be symptomatic of the dysfunctional relationships and events surrounding Christopher – his parents' breakup, Judy's departure to London with Roger, the brief affair between Ed and Mrs Shears (the end of which provoked Ed to kill the dog) – and these are as much the true subject of the novel as Christopher's own drama.

A study of disability

Secondly, and very obviously, the novel is an examination of disability, particularly that form of autism known as Asperger's syndrome. Nowhere in the text are either of these terms used – a *deliberate* omission by the author, who is keen to have us see the world through the eyes of an Asperger's sufferer, rather than simply labelling him and distancing ourselves from his experience. This is the most brilliant part of what Haddon has accomplished. He takes us *inside the head* of a person with a mental disability, but *still* tells a riveting story. As Haddon himself explained in one interview, '[Christopher] is someone whose mind would be a complete closed book if you ever met them and yet part of the magic of a novel is that you slip inside their head straight away' (*Healthcare Customwire*, 14 March 2004)

Deliberately mixed genres

The disparate elements in the text might at first seem odd – like badly matched clothes. However, the strange mix is part of the author's conscious crafting. The worldwide success of the text is a reminder of how original and stimulating it is. As for the 'Rorschach blot' quality (the reader finds in the text what he/she is looking for), Haddon has commented, in what seems a deliberate nod to 'post-modern' thinking about literature:

> Quote
>
> When I first started this book, I thought, 'Oh look – it has layers' … It helps you get immediately into the mind of someone who should be totally closed from you in real life. It's a fiction about … a guy who should be a really bad narrator because he takes everything literally, who doesn't understand emotion and misses the big picture. But he turns out to be a really good narrator because he leaves a lot of space for you to add your own stuff to the story. (*The Independent*, cited above)

The active role of the reader

In short, Haddon implicitly critiques the traditional notion that a text should fit within some genre (or genres), defined by the author, and immutable. He actively accepts, even encourages, the idea that the reader 'makes meaning' out of the fiction, finding elements that are personally relevant, and 'reading' the text in a variety of ways.

Structure

Opening narrative 'hook'

The Curious Incident of the Dog in the Night-time starts with a wonderfully dramatic opening chapter. The 'murder' of Wellington ensures that readers are 'hooked', for as with all whodunnits we then expect to find out who the culprit is. Having opened with such a 'bang', Haddon then has time to unfold his exposition (what we need to know by way of context) in a more leisurely fashion. After letting us know, via Christopher's school writing project, who's who, he picks up on the mystery again. From then on, the story artfully weaves the whodunnit and the personal aspects together.

The beginning of the major change in Christopher

When Christopher finds out that his mother is not dead, but living with Roger Shears in London (Chapter 35, or in Christopher's numbering system '149'), the narrative moves dramatically in another direction. It takes a little time for the evidence of Judy's existence to sink in, and it is not until Chapter 39 ('167') that Christopher finds out about the killing of the dog. By this time, he is deep in crisis, as his vomiting and near catatonic state make clear. However, startled out of his habitual ways of acting, Christopher soon becomes a boy on a mission – to escape his father, and to find his mother again. The epic trek to London – spelled out in torturous detail – leads to the reunion with Judy Boone. This in turn leads to the unravelling of her life with Roger, and the return to Swindon. The book ends with the present of the puppy and tentative reconciliation with Christopher's father.

If we charted this story arc, we could say that at roughly the half-way point in the text (Chapter 37/'157'), the mystery is solved, but the truth prompts a catastrophic shift in Christopher's consciousness, and his personal circumstances. He moves out of his comfort zone, sets out on a (for him) vast journey of discovery and actively tries an alternative life (with his mother). Although

What has changed by the end

he eventually ends up back where he began, he is *not* the same person. He has grown and in a sense triumphed. His discovery goes beyond mere facts. He now knows what his parents are like, and has found in himself inner resources. As the final line says, he realises that '[he] can do anything'.

The novel's unusual numbering system

The novel has the most unusual numbering system ever devised. Christopher chooses to tag his narrative episodes (chapters) not with cardinal numbers (1, 2, 3, etc) but with prime numbers (numbers which are not divisible by any other number except themselves). Here is a table of equivalence, so you can see what is going on:

Christopher's prime number = 2	Standard cardinal number = 1
Christopher's prime number = 3	Standard cardinal number = 2
Christopher's prime number = 5	Standard cardinal number = 3
Christopher's prime number = 7	Standard cardinal number = 4

There are in fact 51 'chapters' in the book, ranging in length from less than one page to 21 pages. The chapters tend to become longer as the text goes on. While it has much to do with the longer narrative fragments once he starts his journey to London, there is also an implied hint that Christopher's mental processes and ability to deal with life are becoming less fragmentary – more coherent and integrated.

One other point might be observed about the text's structure: Haddon is very good at narrative 'pacing'. Take the odd chapter about computers and minds (38/'163') which immediately follows the 'breakdown' chapter (when Christopher realises that his mother is not dead, but living in London). This digression has almost nothing to do with the vomiting scene – except perhaps insofar as it represents a kind of rebuttal by Christopher of the concept of emotions. It is followed in turn by the chronological sequel to the 'breakdown' scene – the story picked up again, as it were. Why Chapter 38? What is it doing there at all? Partly as a clue to Christopher's resistance to the emotions he has just (traumatically) experienced. Partly though just because it allows us a 'breather' – a moment of detensioning, of relief from the trauma. Like Christopher's counting and obsessive puzzle solving when under stress, it is an outlet. Haddon, like any skilled writer, does not rush through the story, giving us a non-stop outpouring of dramatic events. He allows it to proceed in its own time.

A close examination of the text will reveal that Haddon often alternates his main narrative chapters with digressions about the stars, time, perception, the mind, puzzles, and all the things that concern Christopher in his private world. The switching between story and reflection, or speculation, is clever. It not only breaks the forward rush of the narrative, but it tells us a vast amount about Christopher. In short he can be read not just by what he *does*, but by what he *thinks*. Haddon's ability to keep these two dimensions in play, and to unravel his story in a timely way, is another clue to his control over his craft.

Deliberate narrative pacing – the use of 'breather' chapters between dramatic episodes

Story and reflection as constants

Style

A disabled narrator

Christopher is one of the most unusual narrators ever to carry an entire novel (by means of first person narrative) unaided. William Faulkner used the voice of a mentally retarded character in his 1929 masterpiece *The Sound and the Fury* – though the full story is filled in by three other narrators. William Golding told the story of the extinction of the Neanderthals through the eyes of one such creature, in his 1955 work *The Inheritors* – but that is set in a misty prehistory no one has ever seen. Haddon accomplishes something quite extraordinary - he uses a mentally disabled narrator, in a recognisable modern urban setting, and still tells an engrossing story very clearly.

Precedents for this feature

Because Haddon's narrator is autistic, the author sets himself a remarkable challenge. How to make the narrative interesting and 'tangible', while still preserving the sense of Christopher as 'different'? He manages this with masses of detail, verbatim (word for word) dialogue, and a prose style at once weirdly bare and somehow movingly accessible.

The challenge

The style is what we could call 'naïve'. Repeatedly we have 'And I said … And she said … Then she said … And I said …'. Often the sentences go on for some time (in one case for 120 words non-stop) with successive clauses linked only by the conjunction 'and'. In any other book, this would become intolerable. However, because it so perfectly expresses the literal-mindedness of Christopher, it in fact works very well. We have to add our own 'readings' to what Christopher is reporting, simply because he so clearly misses the point, but it is not hard work and it greatly enriches the experience.

The 'naive' style

The way readers add meaning

Related to the issue of why the novel is so accessible, and also under 'style', we need to consider the pictorial elements. There are an astonishing 53 'pictures' in the novel – maps, plans, logos, icons, tables, a photograph, assorted drawings and diagrams (an average of one every five pages!). Why? On the face of it, because the narrative's surface format is well served by them. This is a 15-year-old's 'book', and one with a heightened interest in science and concepts. Christopher does not worry about the convention of no pictures in a 'novel'. He puts in what interests him. More cleverly, Haddon uses the pictures as a way of 'lightening' the text – adding visual dynamism. It is that much more engrossing because we constantly see what is in Christopher's mind. The effect may first startle readers, thought it is also a pleasing novelty.

The many images in the text ... why?

One of the most unusual aspects of the novel stylistically is the 'tragi-comic' feel. Here is a boy whose affliction is quite moving, whose world is full of heartache, yet who is somehow often an accidental clown. Should we feel pity, or should we laugh?

The mixing of comedy and tragedy

One reviewer noted:

> His narrative … is wonderfully funny and deeply sad, even though *he* wouldn't recognise either effect. The humour arises from Chris's interaction with suspects and strangers, and the surreal disconnect – for most of us – between his experiences and his reactions. When fellow passengers [in the trip to London] bump against him, he barks like a dog to warn them off. When a woman at a tube station offers to help him, he says he'll saw off her fingers with his Swiss Army knife if she doesn't stay away. 'OK, buddy,' she replies, 'I'm going to take that as a no.' (*Maclean*'s, 11 August 2003)

The author himself is aware of this tension.

> Humour and high seriousness [are] perfect bedfellows, I think. Though I usually phrase it in terms of comedy and darkness. Comedy without darkness rapidly becomes trivial. And darkness without comedy rapidly becomes unbearable. The comedy and the darkness also allow you to create sentiment without it becoming too sentimental. (Interview with *The Guardian*, 2 February 2004)

Indeed the whole tone of the novel is a strange one. One interviewer summed it up astutely when she said,

> Because Christopher's emotional repertoire does not include self-pity, one rushes in after him, full of sympathy, supplying his deficiencies, doing his feeling for him, filling the void – and this makes the novel emotionally involving in an unusual way. (Kate Kellaway, *The Observer*, 27 April 2003)

We read of Christopher vomiting, barking, groaning, screaming – but because such actions are reported in a matter-of-fact way, without editorialising, there is no melodrama, no special pleading. The book *is* emotionally rich, despite its autistic narrator, and often deeply moving.

Background Notes on Mental Disabilities and Illnesses

The frequency of mental problems

Mental problems are usually divided into two broad classes:

Mental problems associated with brain damage

(1) **Psychiatric (mental) disabilities** are long-term impairments (restrictions or limitations) typically associated with brain damage or cerebral abnormalities. The damage may be the result of genetic conditions (chromosomal abnormalities) – the most common cause; birth trauma (such as a loss of oxygen); accident (now called ABI, or 'acquired brain injury'); or disease (such as Alzheimer's syndrome, a common form of dementia caused by the breakdown of the brain in ageing people).

Common forms of disability

Basically, the many conditions classified under psychiatric disability involve the brains of the subjects not functioning properly (ie within the range of abilities considered 'normal'). These include such conditions as Down's syndrome (once called Mongolism), cerebral palsy (once called being 'spastic'), and the broad umbrella conditions of 'dementia' (in old people) and 'retardation' (which really means exceedingly low cognitive function, ie ability to think) in children and adults.

The number of disabled people in the community

A common measure of intellectual ability is the so-called IQ (Intelligence Quotient), a sometimes controversial concept, though widely recognised. Because of the difficulty of testing people who are severely impaired (for example unable to read or even to speak), there is an element of uncertainty about the figures, but Australian estimates put the figures of school-age children with intellectual disability (IQs of less than 75, when 100 is the median or 'normal' midpoint) at around 0.4% of the general population. As many as 2.3% of all Australians under 65 (1998) were considered to have an intellectual disability of some kind (including impairment of vision, speech, bodily function): that's 377,000 people. A further 126,000 elderly people had mental disabilities: in total 2.5% of the whole population (one in every 40 individuals).

(2) **Mental illnesses** are conditions usually unrelated to IQ (Intelligence Quotient) or to physical impairment. They are still however more or less disabling. Figures from the Department of Health and Aged Care (Canberra) tell us that 'One in five Australians will experience a mental illness [at some stage in their lives]'. Some have a short-lived episode, from which they recover. Others endure the condition throughout their lives. Some are thought to be the result of hereditary predispositions (for instance a family tendency towards schizophrenia). Others are thought to be triggered by trauma, or accident, or drugs.

Common mental illnesses include:

* depression – a long-term state of melancholia, going very much beyond the 'normal' feelings of sadness experienced by all people after a disappointment or stressful event. In extreme cases, it can be life threatening if not treated, because of the risk of suicide. The good news? It can be effectively treated with either medication or cognitive therapy, or both.

* bipolar mood disorder (formerly called manic depression) – characterised by periods of 'mania' (unnatural elation and hyperactivity), followed by periods of depression: two in every hundred people experience the disorder. It can be effectively controlled with drugs.

* anxiety disorder – characterised by persistent feelings of high anxiety, including panic attacks, usually without discernible cause. This condition effectively disables the sufferer. Phobias (extreme fears), such as agoraphobia (fear of being in any open space with other people) and obsessive compulsive disorder (constant unwanted thoughts, or repetitive rituals such as endlessly washing one's hands) are common variants. About one in 20 people at any given time experience anxiety disorder. It can be treated effectively with either medication or cognitive therapy, or both.

* eating disorders – such as anorexia (starving oneself), bulimia (eating binges followed by self-induced vomiting, or compulsive exercise) and obsessive cyclical dieting. About 2% of teenage girls suffer from anorexia. These disorders can be quite dangerous, despite the perception that they are trivial (and self-induced). However, with treatment, they can be overcome.

International figures vary widely, with USA estimates of 20% for adult mental disorders in one survey and 29% in another survey. These are the highest in the developed world. Australian figures are nearly 18% for adults (18+) and 14% for children (up to 17). The major illnesses are depression (5% of the Australian population) and schizophrenia (perhaps around 0.4% of the total population).

Asperger's syndrome

This is a mild form of autism – from the Greek word for 'self' (referring to individuals trapped within a private world). Unlike classic 'low functioning' autism (which afflicts around 0.2% of the population), whose victims often suffer from mental retardation, and are totally unable to function independently, Asperger's children usually have normal or even high IQs. Also called 'high functioning autism', it is one of the 'Pervasive Developmental Disorders' (PDDs), where there is severe disruption of the 'normal' mental growth of a child. The disorder is more common in boys than girls. It is generally diagnosed between the ages of 5 and 9. It is a lifelong condition and there is no cure. The syndrome is named after Dr Hans Asperger, a Viennese pediatrician, who gave it its first clinical description in 1944.

Asperger's: 'high functioning' autism

Individuals with 'Asperger's' have major impairment of social interaction skills. They tend to be 'smart' and have good verbal abilities, but they have trouble understanding emotions and relating to other people. Nonverbal cues (body language and tone) are meaningless to them. They typically avoid eye contact and touching. They often have difficulty with sensory processing (ie dealing with the sights, sounds and other stimuli we take for granted), and experience 'overload' quite easily. Needless to say this is a huge impediment and causes real suffering. School (if they attend it) is a nightmare. They are often bullied and treated as freaks. Of one child with the syndrome, a carer said 'Yes he *did* want to go to school, but he wished that all the other children weren't there'. Even family relationships are difficult. Asperger's children tend to have no friends. They inhabit a private world of intellectual speculation or fantasy. They usually have highly exotic interests – often of a scientific or technical nature (cars, trains, French literature, meteorology, astronomy, etc). One resource calls it 'the geek syndrome', referring to the fact that many sufferers are clever 'boffins' – brilliant with computers or maths. They are obsessed with numbers and order. If their routines are disrupted

Symptoms of Asperger's syndrome

or they are threatened with new situations, they can become panic-stricken and/or angry.

The positive side of Asperger's

Although life is extremely difficult for people with Asperger's, they usually have jobs and leave relatively satisfactory lives. The lucky ones tend to find their niche in areas like engineering, mathematics and computer programming, where obsessive concern with detail and a 'loner' mentality is acceptable. One study suggests that the condition is endemic in 'Silicon Valley' (the IT 'capital' of America), where they find an outlet for their difference in the highly specialised realms of software development and Artificial Intelligence.

What needs to be done?

Because of the stigma (literally black mark or brand) attached to mental illness, many people with mental health difficulties are in double jeopardy: they have to endure their condition, *and* they have to put up with the fear, contempt or even outright mockery of those with whom they come in contact. Common misconceptions include the following:

Popular myths about mental illness and disability

*   people with mental illness are dangerous (normally they are completely harmless)
*   people with mental illness got that way because of drugs (only a tiny percentage may have been caused by substance abuse – the vast majority suffer from hereditary problems)
*   people with mental illness can cure themselves if they just exercise some willpower and try harder (conscious self-modification is not an option for most sufferers – a condition like Asperger's is effectively 'hard wired' into them)
*   people with mental illness should be locked away for their safety and to keep the community safe (most conditions can be 'managed', and only a tiny percentage of patients need hospital care)
*   people with mental illness are doomed to be that way for life: it depends on the illness – some can be successfully treated, and the sufferer lead a normal life; others are disabling over a long time, but even there modern medical science and enlightened health policy has devised ways to optimise the lives of those affected.

Summary and Commentary

NB: In the following summary, the 'chapters' are numbered sequentially in the traditional manner, but Christopher's prime number titles (the ones used in the book) are added in brackets.

Chapter 1 (2)

Christopher discovers Wellington

The unnamed narrator (Christopher) discovers the body of Wellington, Mrs Shears' poodle. The dog has been killed with a garden fork. Christopher is mystified.

> *Quote*
>
> I stroked Wellington and wondered who had killed him, and why.

Chapter 2 (3)

Christopher introduces himself. He tells the reader that he knows every capital city in the world and all the prime numbers up to 7,507. However, he has trouble with feelings. He recognises the sad face (icon) that Siobhan (his teacher) drew for him, and knows he felt that when he found Wellington. He recognises the happy face, and relates 'happiness' to his hobbies and being alone. But he is confused by other faces (ironic, confused, surprised, etc).

Chapter 3 (5)

Mrs Shears accuses Christopher

Christopher takes the fork out of the dead dog and hugs him. At this moment, Mrs Shears comes running out of the house, shouting **'What ... have you done to my dog?'** When she starts screaming, Christopher rolls onto the grass with his hands over his ears and his eyes closed.

Chapter 4 (7)

Christopher announces that this is to be **'a murder mystery novel'**, which he is writing because Siobhan has encouraged him to write something *he* would want to read. He does not like **'proper novels'** because he cannot understand them. But he likes mysteries because they are puzzles which can be solved. His involves a dog murder, not a human murder, but then he likes dogs because they are **'faithful and honest'**.

Chapter 5 (11)

The policeman questions Christopher

The police arrive. While Mrs Shears is led back inside the house by a policewoman, a policeman questions Christopher about his involvement. Christopher feels that **'he [is] asking too many questions ... too quickly'**, and gets down on the ground again, **'groaning'**. He explains

> Quote
>
> I make this noise when there is too much information coming into my head from the outside world.

Christopher hits him

When the policeman goes to lift him up, Christopher (who doesn't like being touched), hits the policeman.

Chapter 6 (13)

Christopher denies that this will be a funny book. He cannot understand jokes. He tells one, and (laboriously) explains what is supposed to make it funny.

Chapter 7 (17)

Christopher is arrested and taken to the police station

The policeman arrests Christopher, who is now much calmer. They drive off in the police car. Christopher looks up at the Milky Way. He explains where our Sun fits into it, and how the expanding universe stops the night sky being full of starlight. He then adds that when the universe has stopped expanding, it will collapse again – though no one will be alive to see it.

Chapter 8 (19)

Christopher explains that he has chosen to number the chapters in his book with prime numbers. He explains what prime numbers are and how useful they are. He likes them.

I think prime numbers are like life. They are very logical but you could never work out the rules, even if you spent all your time thinking about them.

Chapter 9 (23)

Christopher is put in a cell

At the police station, Christopher is made to hand over the contents of his pockets (described one by one), although they leave him his watch when he screams (at the thought of not knowing exactly what time it was). They ask him about his family, and he gives them his father's phone numbers. He is put in a small cell, and spends the time thinking about methods of escape. He wonders if Mrs Shears has lied about him killing Wellington.

Chapter 10 (29)

Christopher confesses, **'I find people confusing'**. This is because of **'talking without using any words'** (body language) and because of metaphors. He gives examples of both. He moves to the meaning of his own name – derived from St Christopher (one who carries Christ) – but he does not want his name to mean a story: **'I want my name to mean me'**.

Chapter 11 (31)

Father gets Christopher out of jail

'Father' arrives at the police station, angrily demanding to see Christopher. When they are reunited, he and Christopher touch fingers in a fan shape (the only touch Christopher can abide). An inspector questions Christopher, and then issues him with a 'caution' (official warning). They leave the police station.

Chapter 12 (37)

Christopher states that **'I do not tell lies'**, not because he is a good person (as 'Mother' claimed), but because **'I can't tell lies'**. He explains that a lie is saying something happened that didn't happen. He admits to a feeling of panic when he starts thinking about all the possibilities in the world, which is why he sticks to the truth.

Chapter 13 (41)

Father orders Christopher to forget the dog

On the way home, Christopher's father tells him he has to stay out of trouble. When Christopher asserts that he is going to find out who killed the dog, Father says **'It's a bloody dog'**. When Christopher continues, his father shouts **'I said leave it, for God's sake'**.

Back home, Christopher feeds his pet rat (Toby) and plays on his computer. He sees his father crying. **'Are you sad about Wellington?'** he asks. Christopher leaves his father alone.

Commentary

The ostensible subject of the 'novel' is the 'murder mystery' – the 'whodunnit' case involving dead Wellington, announced in the first chapter. It *is* indeed a strong opening, obeying Siobhan's rule that a novel 'should begin with something to grab people's attention'.

However, it soon becomes clear that the author is playing a more complicated game. The following chapters reveal that the *real* subject of the novel is to be something else. The clues are too obvious to ignore. The narrator (Christopher) first collapses in a type of fit (induced by Mrs Shears' screaming), then strikes the policeman, then is arrested and jailed, and only escapes by the intervention of his long-suffering father. We realise that the 'murder' of Wellington is merely a scene-grabbing opening gambit. The *true* subject of the novel is Christopher *himself*. After all, his actions are not normal ones. The 'groaning', the fear of being touched, the panic at not having his watch, the obsessive detailing and explanations – above all his bizarre emotional detachment from what is going on (eg he can discourse on the night sky while being taken to the police station) – suggest some-one with a mental disability.

Nowhere in the text does Haddon ever mention the words 'autism' or 'Asperger's syndrome', but these clearly underlie Christopher's behaviour. We begin to put the pieces of the puzzle together from the naïve fragments of information he provides: the lack of understanding of emotions (Chapters 2 and 10, and most poignantly, 13, not understanding why his father is crying), the literalism, the indications that he is a 'savant' (maths, astronomy, geography) – are all classic symptoms of Asperger's.

It is *very* important to recognise that Christopher is *not* stupid. Far from it, he is uncommonly clever – but his blind spots (emotion, touching, understanding human interactions) are crippling. He can read books, even write one – but he cannot read people. He lacks a grasp of subtext, or human psychology. He lacks the flexibility and adaptability to circumstances that everyday existence demands. For example, in a world where little white lies are expected, are considered normal (as for instance when the inspector tries to get Christopher to say that what he did was an 'accident'), not being able to lie is a serious disability.

He is not the *only* one with a problem, though. While the text foregrounds Christopher, we have tantalising clues about other problems. Who killed the dog, for instance? We don't perhaps see this as a *Hound of the Baskervilles* level case, but we do realise that it points to someone (in Christopher's world) acting very badly. There is the reaction of Mrs Shears. There is his father's weeping. Above all, there is the major clue that his mother is dead ('Mother was a small person ...'). We wait to see how these mysteries will unfold, along with the central one of Christopher himself.

Chapter 14 (43)

Christopher recalls the 'death' of his mother

'Mother died 2 years ago,' says Christopher. He recalls how one day when he came home no one was there. His father looked around for Christopher's mother, and then went out. When he returned, he said **'I'm afraid you won't be seeing your mother for a while'**. Christopher noted that **'he didn't look at me when he said this'**. Christopher was told that his mother had **'a problem with her heart'** and was in hospital.

Chapter 15 (47)

'Good days' and 'bad days'

Christopher recalls that the next day it was a 'Good Day'. He knew this because they had passed four red cars in a row on the way to school. He explains, **'I liked things to be in a nice order'**, which made him **'feel safe'**. Yellow cars, however, meant a 'Black Day', and then he would not speak to anyone. He had discussed these things with Mr Jeavons, the school psychologist. Christopher admitted that he wouldn't mind change if it meant becoming an astronaut, though Mr Jeavons counselled him about how difficult it was to become an astronaut. Christopher recalled an older boy telling him he would only ever get a job collecting supermarket trollies because **'they didn't let spazzers drive rockets'**. Christopher however knows he is not a 'spazzer', and that he intends to go to university, to study mathematics.

Christopher decides to investigate

Because it was a Good Day, Christopher decided he would try to find out who killed Wellington. Siobhan suggested he write about the Wellington incident – hence the book.

Chapter 16 (53)

More about the death of Christopher's mother

'Mother died two weeks later,' Christopher reports. He had sent her a Get Well card with lots of red cars on it (making it a Super Super Good Day). Father told Christopher that she had died of a heart attack. When Christopher asked what sort, because she was only 38 and healthy, his father refused to answer. Christopher speculated about the possibility that it was an aneurysm or maybe an embolism.

Mrs Shears (the neighbour) came over and cooked supper for them. **She 'held [Father's] head against her bosoms and said, "Come on, Ed. We're going to get you through this."'**

Chapter 17 (59)

Christopher decides *not* to obey his father's command: **'Stay out of other people's business'**. This is because it is non-specific, unlike Siobhan's highly detailed instructions, and because his father breaks rules all the time.

Christopher visits Mrs Shears and checks the garden shed

That evening, he visits Mrs Shears to tell her he did not kill Wellington. She shuts the door on him.

He investigates, checking her garden shed, where he sees a fork exactly like that used to kill Wellington. She tells him to leave or she will call the police.

Chapter 18 (61)

Christopher reports that Mrs Forbes (at school) told him when his mother died that she had gone to heaven. But Christopher knows that heaven does not exist.

I think people believe in heaven because they don't like the idea of dying, because they want to carry on living and they don't like the idea that other people will move into their house and put their things into the rubbish.

He explains the process of rotting, using Rabbit as an example. His mother, however, was cremated, he tells us.

Chapter 19 (67)

As part of his detective work, Christopher draws up a plan of the neighbours' houses, and heads off to investigate. He regards this as 'brave', because he is generally scared of strangers.

Christopher interviews the neigh-bours

He interviews Mr Thompson at number 40, who is rude, a black lady at number 44, who advises him not to ask such questions, Mr Wise at number 43, who laughs at him, and old Mrs Alexander at number 39. She engages him in conversation, and offers him cake and a drink. She is gone so long, however, that he gets nervous, and walks away.

Mr Shears the Prime Suspect

Christopher deduces that Wellington was probably killed by someone known to Mrs Shears, and finally arrives at the conclusion that Mr Shears is the 'Prime Suspect'. Mr Shears lived with his wife until two years ago, at which time he left. Mrs Shears would come over to Christopher's house and cook for him and his father, and sometimes even stay the night.

Chapter 20 (71)

Christopher's school – and his ambitions

'All the other children at my school are stupid,' announces Christopher, dismissing the polite euphemism 'Special Needs'. He is about to do his A level in Maths (equivalent of Year 12 VCE), after special pleading by his father. He intends to go on to university and get a degree in Maths or Physics.

Chapter 21 (73)

Christopher's Behavioural Problems

Christopher remembers thinking that his mother and father might get divorced, because of the number of arguments they had. He adds, **'This was because of the stress of looking after someone**

who has Behavioural Problems like I have'. He then lists his behavioural problems, which include

> Not talking to people ... Not eating or drinking ... Not liking being touched ... Screaming when I am angry or confused ... Not liking being in really small places with other people ... Smashing things ... Groaning ... Not liking yellow things or brown things ... Not eating food if different sorts of food are touching each other ... Not noticing that people are angry with me ... Not smiling ... Hitting other people ...

These things made his mother and father **'really angry'**.

Chapter 22 (79)

When Christopher gets home, his father tells him about a phone call from Mrs Shears. Christopher admits he was **'doing detective work'** and mentions Mr Shears as a suspect. His father gets very angry. He describes Mr Shears as 'evil' and Mrs Shears as 'not a friend any more'. He makes Christopher promise to **'stop this ridiculous bloody detective game right now'**. Christopher promises.

Father again warns Christopher off the case

Chapter 23 (83)

Christopher declares that he would make a very good astronaut, because he is intelligent, understands how machines work and likes being in small spaces (as long as he is alone). He would not be homesick as he would be surrounded by **'things I like, which are machines and computers and outer space'**, and would be able to look at the stars. It would be **'a Dream Come True'**.

Chapter 24 (89)

At school, Christopher shows what he has written to Siobhan, who tells him the book is really good. He feels it is not a proper book **'because it didn't have a proper ending because I never found out who killed Wellington so the murderer was still At Large'**. They discuss Mr and Mrs Shears and his father's falling out with them.

The following two days are Black Days (because of the yellow

Christopher and Siobhan

cars Christopher sees). On the second day, Christopher **'sat in the corner of the Library groaning with my head pressed into the join between the two walls and this made me feel calm and safe'**.

Chapter 25 (97)

Mrs Alexander offers information about Mrs Shears

The next day however is a 'Super Good Day', and Christopher expects something special to happen. He meets Mrs Alexander in a shop and they talk, though he declares **'I can't do chatting'**. Being careful not to break the literal sense of his father's rules, he asks her about Mr Shears. Mrs Alexander advises him not to ask, adding **'I think you know why your father doesn't like Mr Shears very much'**. He asks her what she means. They take a walk in the park, and she tells him, **'Your mother, before she died, was very good friends with Mr Shears...Very, very good friends'**. **'Do you mean that they were doing sex?'** he asks, and she confirms that they were. Christopher goes home.

Commentary

While again Christopher's 'murder' investigation is the vehicle that drives the narrative, in fact what emerges is more the human story of a boy with 'behavioural problems' and the dramatic effects these have on his confused parents. Christopher's naïve, emotionless reportage gives little sense of the chaos in the Boone household, but enough detail is provided to let us know that life with him has been extremely difficult. Despite his high intelligence, he is subject to the obsessive and anti-social behaviour characteristic of 'high functioning autism'.

Our first reaction might be to see the comedy in the situation, but what is really laid bare is a family torn apart by disability. Though Christopher cannot see the connections, we now understand that the affair his mother had with Mr Shears was a key moment in the breakdown of relations, and in parallel, for a time, there was an affair between Ed Boone and Mrs Shears, though they have now fallen out acrimoniously. With Mr Shears absent, although Christopher cannot yet see it, his own father becomes a 'prime suspect' regarding the death of Wellington.

If we are reading carefully between the lines, we might also begin to suspect the sudden death of Christopher's mother. We might recall his father's averted eyes, the lack of any contact between the boy and his mother in hospital, the fact that the death was only reported (*not* witnessed directly), and the mystery cremation. What had this to do with the calamitous state of affairs in the Boone and Shears families? Perhaps a great deal. Like most good mysteries, we are presented with enough information to keep us guessing, without yet having the final solution. Ironically, *we* now understand much more about what really happened than *Christopher*.

We also by now have a much clearer idea of Christopher himself. We see the problem side, which he candidly catalogues for us (21/'73'). We also see the upside – his high intelligence (to do a pre-university maths exam at age 15 bespeaks extraordinary talent), his genuine attempts to fit in and be 'good', his quite loveable innocence. Is Christopher an anti-hero? Perhaps. But he is a very sympathetic one.

Our growing sense of identification with this unusual protagonist is one of the miracles of the text: we are beginning to see the world through the eyes of an autistic character, and, far from rejecting or pitying him, feel the relative validity of his point of view. In the 'metanarrative' of the text (ie what the text is *really* doing, 'behind' the story itself), this pushes us towards understanding and tolerance, and does so far more powerfully and subtly than any number of essays or reports on the disabled. It is one of Haddon's most striking achievements.

Chapter 26 (101)

Mr Jeavon believes Christopher likes maths because **'it was safe'**. Christopher adds that

> Quote
>
> what he meant was that maths wasn't like life because in life there are no straightforward answers at the end.

Christopher and maths

Christopher then gives a lengthy example of the tension between intuition and logic, citing a maths problem called the Monty Hall Problem – about a hypothetical TV game show with three doors and the chance of winning a goat or a car by picking a particular door. Christopher demonstrates that the problem can be solved by strict mathematical logic.

Chapter 27 (103)

Christopher calculates in his head

At home, Christopher is questioned by his father about what he has been doing. He answers evasively. His father's employee Rhodri sets him a mathematical problem: 'What's 251 times 864?' Christopher immediately does the maths in his head and answers correctly.

Christopher then adds in a description of the sky, detailing the shape of a cloud which looks like an alien spaceship. He discusses what aliens would look like if they exist.

Chapter 28 (107)

Christopher and Sherlock Holmes

Christopher's favourite book is *The Hound of the Baskervilles*. In it, Sherlock Holmes solves the mystery of the mythical hound, and identifies the criminal behind the deception. Christopher lists some of the clues in the story, and some 'Red Herrings'. He identifies with Sherlock Holmes, who **'had, in a very remarkable degree, the power of detaching his mind at will'**. Christopher compares his own book to Holmes' investigations.

Chapter 29 (109)

Christopher shows his work to Siobhan, who asks him 'Did it make you upset to find out that your mother and Mr Shears had an affair?' to which Christopher replies simply 'No'. He explains, **'Because Mother is dead. And because Mr Shears isn't around any more'**.

Chapter 30 (113)

Christopher and the concept of memory

Christopher discusses memory, and how he stores details about people and events, so that he can 'search' for a match if required. He recalls an incident at the beach when he was nine, and how he screamed when his mother disappeared (temporarily) under the water in the sea. He recalls a comment made by his mother about who she might have married. He mentions Siobhan talking about imagining a happy scene if she is depressed, but he is unable to imagine things about his mother, because she is dead.

Chapter 31 (127)

*Father
discovers
the journal:
they fight*

Christopher leaves his book (the journal account of what he has been doing) on the kitchen table, while he goes to watch a video about the sea. His father comes home and reads the book. He flies into a rage and grabs Christopher by the arm. Christopher loses control and hits his father, repeatedly. He reports

> I had no memories for a short while ... It was like someone had switched me off and then switched me on again. And when they switched me on again I was sitting on the carpet with my back against the wall and there was blood on my right hand and the side of my head was hurting.

Christopher's father drops the book into the dustbin outside.

Chapter 32 (131)

Christopher explains why he hates yellow and brown.

Chapter 33 (137)

At the zoo

The following day, Christopher's father apologises, and takes him to Twycross Zoo (as a special treat). Over lunch, his father says

> I love you very much, Christopher. Don't ever forget that. And I know I lose my rag occasionally. I know I get angry. I know I shout. And I know I shouldn't. But I only do it because I worry about you, because I don't want to see you getting into trouble, because I don't want you to get hurt. Do you understand?

*Apology and
reconciliation*

He stretches out his hand and they touch fingers. Christopher draws a map of the zoo.

Chapter 34 (139)

Christopher admits that while he likes Sherlock Holmes, he does *not* admire (author) Sir Arthur Conan Doyle. This is because Doyle lost a son in the war, and joined the Spiritualist Society, hoping to

Christopher's problem with Arthur Conan Doyle

speak with the dead boy (via a spirit medium). Furthermore, Doyle believed in the 'Cottingley Fairies', a hoax perpetuated by two girls who took fake pictures of fairies with their father's camera.

Christopher relates this hoax to 'Occam's razor', the scientific principle which argues that **'No more things should be presumed to exist than are absolutely necessary'**, and in turn to the killer of Wellington (someone known to the victim).

Chapter 35 (149)

At school, Siobhan asks Christopher about the bruise on his face. He tells her about the fight with his father, but shows no fear of going home again, so Siobhan lets the matter lapse.

Christopher searches for and finds his book

When he returns home, Christopher goes to the dustbin and looks for his book, but it isn't there. He then looks inside the house, 'detecting' in various places, methodically. Eventually he ends up in his father's room, where he finds the missing book (in a shirt box in the cupboard). He hears his father returning home, and is just about to leave when he sees an envelope with his name on it. He takes it with him. Later, he looks at it.

The letter from his 'dead' mother

It is a letter from his mother, telling him about her new job in London. He looks at the postmark and sees that it was posted **'18 months after Mother had died'**. Christopher realises that now he has *two* mysteries to solve. He decides to wait until his father is out of the house, and then look at the other letters which are in the box.

Chapter 36 (151)

'Lots of things are mysteries,' says Christopher. He uses the example of ghosts, and of a pond at school with frogs. He analyses the frog population in the pond mathematically, showing that it becomes 'chaotic' under certain conditions.

Chapter 37 (157)

Christopher reads his mother's letters

A week later, Christopher has the opportunity to revisit his father's bedroom and look at more of the letters. He reads them (and they are reproduced in the text). The letters from his mother reveal a whole new life that she is living in London, with Roger Shears. She confesses that **'I was not a very good mother'** and reminds him of how she reacted on one occasion when he had a fit while they were out shopping. She admits that she and his father had fights, in one of which **'I said I couldn't take it [living with Christopher's disability] anymore'**. She explains that she started spending time with Roger. One night she and Christopher had an argument and she ended up in hospital.

> And I think that was when I realised you and your father were probably better off if I wasn't living in the house. Then he would only have one person to look after instead of two.

She explains that Roger got a transfer and asked her to accompany him to London.

> I meant to say goodbye ... But when I rang your father he said I couldn't come back. He was really angry. He said I couldn't talk to you ... He said ... that I was never to set foot inside the house again. So I haven't. But I have written you these letters instead.

The letter ends with her begging him to get in touch with her.

Christopher understands the truth at last, and collapses

Other letters tell Christopher about her new job, and other details of her life. Christopher writes, **'Then I stopped reading the letter because I felt sick'**. He understands what has happened at last.

He curls up on the bed, and loses consciousness. He vomits.

Later, he hears his father calling his name. His father comes into the room and is angry. Then he realises, and weeps.

> I did it for your good, Christopher. Honestly I did. I never meant to lie. I just thought ... it was better if you didn't know.

Father tries to explain

He explains that the lie about her being in hospital 'got out of control'. He runs a bath for Christopher, and gently leads him to it.

Commentary

It has taken until just over half-way through the text before Christopher discovers the truth about his mother. Haddon's use of 'dramatic irony' (the gap between what *readers* understand and what a *character* understands) is very clever. We have long since begun to suspect the truth, and Chapter 35 ('149') confirms it. Yet it still takes another two chapters before the reality becomes clear to *Christopher*. His understanding that his father has lied, that his mother is *not* dead but living in London, and that he has been kept away from her for whole two years – hits him with such force that he is physically ill. It is a kind of mini 'breakdown'. The fact that we do not have a dramatic retelling of this trauma (because the narrator does not have such narrative skills) cannot take away from the savagery of the experience.

Yet this painful moment is also cathartic (cleansing). What Christopher doesn't understand, but *we* do, is that what has broken over him is a tidal wave of emotion – his longing for his mother, his horror at what his father has done. Because Christopher cannot cope with emotion, he vomits and becomes incapacitated. But the expression of these emotions is necessary. It is nothing less than the pain we *have* to feel – the other side of love – when people we care for (and are dependent on) hurt us. Christopher's normal coping mechanisms – shutting out feelings and 'illogical' elements – can no longer sustain him. His autistic isolation has been shattered, and though it is extremely distressing, it represents a new phase – one in which he is able to be more 'engaged' or connected than before. Significantly, too, that pain and sense of loss is to provide him with the motivation for the epic quest he will shortly begin.

Although Christopher is the centre of our attention in Chapter 37 ('157'), it is also worth thinking about Ed Boone here too. Although it is tempting to cast Ed as the villain, and see his lies about the mother as despicable, there is more to it. Judy Boone herself acknowledges, in the letter, that Christopher's father coped better with the boy than *she* did. And even in this scene, which is quite wrenching, Ed comes across as a man who genuinely cares. He weeps, he apologises, he gently leads Christopher off to clean him up. These are not the actions of a brute, but of a father who is trying to make amends. In his portrayal of both parents, Haddon is showing us ordinary people, both highly flawed, who find coping with a person like Christopher very difficult. There are no false heroics here – just the banal, painful realities of living with a disabled individual.

Chapter 38 (163)

The mind as a machine

Christopher argues that **'the mind is just a complicated machine'**. People can have pictures on the 'screens' inside their heads – seeing what happened in the past or what might happen – and they carry around images of themselves in their heads. But although people think they are quite different from computers, says Christopher, in truth they are not.

Chapter 39 (167)

Christopher, still in a post-traumatic stupor, looks at his knees and doubles 2s in his head (to try and keep calm), while his father cleans up and offers him food. Father apologises again, saying *Father confesses about Wellington* **'Life is difficult ... It's bloody hard telling the truth all the time'**, and then adds **'I killed Wellington, Christopher'**. He proceeds to explain how he and Mrs Shears were 'friends', but then had some rows and he began to realise that they (he and Christopher) were less important to her than the dog. After one of these rows, Wellington was 'waiting for me' and **'that red mist [came] down ... [and] everything I'd been bottling up for two years just [came out]'**. He concludes, hopelessly, **'we're not that different, you and me'**.

But Christopher is convinced that **'he [Father] could murder *Christopher, fearful, runs away* me, because I couldn't trust him'**. Christopher waits a long time, then gets Toby (in his cage), puts on coats, goes quietly out to the shed in the back yard, and hides.

Chapter 40 (173)

Christopher looks up at the stars, and thinks about the names of the constellations.

Chapter 41 (179)

Christopher stays hidden until morning. His father comes out and calls, but Christopher does not reply. His father drives off.

Christopher decides he must go to London and find Mother	Christopher tries to work out what he will do. After considering all the options, he decides that he should go to London to live with his mother. He thinks about physical pain that he has experienced, but realises that **'this hurt was inside my head'**. However, he 'Formulated a Plan', which makes him feel better.

He goes to Mrs Alexander, and asks her if she will look after Toby for him when he goes to London. He tells her what he has discovered. She suggests getting in touch with his father, so he runs off. He returns home, collects food and, finding his father's credit card, puts it in his pocket. He puts Toby in his pocket, and heads off. His fear of new places and experiences is balanced by his fear of his father.

He makes his way to the station

He walks to the school, but his father's van is there. Christopher vomits again, but calms himself (with difficulty). He then asks a lady for directions to the station. He follows a bus going by, and after much searching, locates the station.

Chapter 42 (181)

Christopher's all-seeing perception

Christopher explains that **'I see everything'**, describing how his observations of people and places is not 'glancing' (like most people), but a detailed categorising of *all* the objects in view. He gives the example of the many details he saw when he stopped in a field with cows (years earlier). He adds,

> Quote
>
> When I am in a new place, because I see everything, it is like when a computer is doing too many things at the same time and the central processor unit is blocked up and there isn't any space left to think about other things ... [so when in a new place] it is like a computer crashing and I have to close my eyes and put my hands over my ears and groan ...

Commentary

The trauma leads to a momentous shift. Unable to face his father any more, Christopher is motivated to seek an alternative. That means confronting his fears, and leaving his comfort zone. Although the actions he then takes are, by *our* standards, minimal, they are, for *Christopher*, of mammoth proportions. The simple business of going to the railway station is a major undertaking, beset with confusion and fear. The fact that he has never been there before is a reminder of how protected his life has been, and when we see his reactions in the street, we remember why.

Nonetheless, fearful or not, Christopher is off on a journey of discovery. The outward physical movements are in many ways symbolic of the inner psychological movement. He is now acting independently, and finding his own way. This, for an autistic child, is a huge risk. But the potential benefits, which *we* can sense (if he cannot) far outweigh the dangers.

Chapter 43 (191)

At the station, Christopher confronts his fears (of strangers, noise and a new place) and forces himself to walk through the tunnel (under the railway lines) to the station cafeteria. He does a complicated maths problem called 'Conway's Soldiers' to calm himself.

Christopher and the policeman

A policeman appears (he has been called by the café manager) and asks Christopher what he is doing. The truth gradually emerges. The policeman goes with him to an automatic teller machine, where Christopher withdraws twenty pounds for the ticket to London. Christopher goes to the ticket window and, trying to keep calm, buys a ticket. Still fighting down his fear, and trying to pretend it is all a computer game, Christopher makes his way to the platform and boards the train.

He boards the train

Chapter 44 (193)

Christopher explains how he likes timetables. He recalls one he made of his daily routine, before discussing the larger problem of past and future, and the relativity of time. He likes timetables, which are 'maps of time', because **'they make sure you don't get lost in time'**.

Chapter 45 (197)

Christopher 'caught'

Christopher is surprised by the policeman, who announces that his father is at the police station. He suggests Christopher and his father 'sit down and have a little chat'. Just as he is about to compel Christopher, the train pulls out of the station. The police-man radios for a car to meet them at the next stop. Time goes by.

Christopher needs to go to the toilet, and accidentally wets himself. The policeman angrily sends Christopher off to the toilet. Afterwards, he climbs into a luggage rack and conceals himself with a suitcase. The policeman comes looking for him, but can't find him, and gets off the train. The train pulls out of the station.

He escapes

Chapter 46 (199)

God

'People believe in God because the world is very complicated and they think it is very unlikely that anything as complicated as a flying squirrel or the human eye or a brain could happen by chance,' says Christopher, before explaining that chance in fact rules the universe. Human beings, he asserts, are not in fact special, and *could* make themselves extinct.

Chapter 47 (211)

In London, Christopher tries to find his way

The train finally arrives at (Paddington Station) London. Christopher is found by several people, but they go away again. He gets off the train. When he sees a policeman, he leaves the platform as quickly as he can. He sees all the signs (reproduced in the text), which are a frightening jumble to him. He goes to an information office, and the lady there tells him to take the 'tube' (Underground railway) to Willesden Green or Junction. Christopher makes his way down into the Underground and works out how to buy a ticket at an automatic ticket machine. Slowly and painfully, he deduces how to get to Willesden Junction. He makes his way through the tunnels and onto the platform leading to Willesden Junction. He sits on a bench and sees the platform fill with people, and the trains coming and going. Overcome with the noise and chaos, he cannot do anything at all. Time goes by, and he continues to sit there.

Trapped in the Under-ground

Chapter 48 (223)

Christopher inserts another 'description', this time of an adver-tisement for a holiday in Malaysia which he sees on the station wall. He can't understand however why people would want to **'go**

on holidays to see new things and relax', when there are so many interesting things to discover without going anywhere.

Chapter 49 (227)

Rescuing Toby (a near-death experience)

Time goes by. The number of people and trains diminishes. Christopher has been sitting there for five hours. Suddenly, he realises that Toby is missing. He looks, and finally sees the rat 'in the lower-down bit where the rails were'. Christopher climbs down off the platform and goes after Toby, but he runs away. Christopher catches him, but just then a train comes into the station. He is rescued in the nick of time by a stranger, who pulls him to safety.

Some time later, Christopher gets onto a train, and it takes him through a number of stations, until he gets to Willesden Junction. Christopher gets off. He asks a man in a little shop how to get to the address of his mother. The man sells him a London A–Z Street Atlas. With some difficulty, Christopher finds the address. No one is home, so he sits down to wait.

Christopher finds Mother

Late at night, he hears voices approaching **'And the lady's voice was Mother's voice'**. She embraces him, to his discomfort, and asks him what happened.

> And I said, 'I'm going to live with you because Father killed Wellington with a garden fork and I'm frightened of him.

She (and Roger Shears) take Christopher inside, and she runs him a bath. She asks him why he didn't write to her, and he explains. She weeps, and tries (in vain) to hold his hand.

They are interrupted by the arrival of a policeman. He questions Christopher and his mother, and then goes away. Christopher goes to bed.

Father appears

In the middle of the night, Christopher hears his father's voice. There is a loud verbal fight between the parents, and then Ed comes into the room where Christopher is. He apologises again:

> Christopher, I'm really, really sorry. About every-thing. About Wellington. About the letters. About making you run away. I never meant ... I promise I will never do anything like that again. Hey. Come on, kiddo.

But despite his father's tears, Christopher refuses to touch him. The policeman returns, and Christopher's father is escorted out.

Chapter 50 (229)

Christopher's dream of an empty Earth

Christopher has a favourite dream. This one is about a fantasy in which everyone on the Earth is dead because of a mysterious virus spread by the meaning of what people say with their faces – leaving only **'special people like me'** alive – people who don't want to touch and ask questions. Christopher dreams of wandering the empty streets, playing without restriction. In his dream, Christopher drives down the street and goes to the empty beach. In the dream, he is happy.

Commentary

The journey to London is a magnificent example of how the author recreates the mental world of his protagonist. The meaning of Christopher's achievement can hardly be missed. As one reviewer put it:

> Quote
>
> [Christopher] responds [to the crisis] courageously, summoning all his willpower to travel from his hometown of Swindon to London, a 150 km journey by rail and subway that's as harrowing for him as Frodo's trek to Mordor [in *Lord of the Rings*]. (*Macleans*, cited above)

The screaming of the Underground trains (as they come into the station), the suffocating crowds, the threatening (to his mind) attentions of other people, the near-death experience on the train track (which he only half understands for what it is), represent horrors of major proportions. Yet, although it takes time, Christopher struggles with his fear and gradually masters the challenges. He finally achieves his goal and finds his mother.

For readers, no doubt, the reunion is a very moving one. However, for Christopher, it is just a task that he has accomplished. The mismatch between *his* reaction, and *hers*, is a subtle reminder of how difficult his condition is. If we need further reminding, it comes in the form of the virus dream – a poignantly sad fantasy. We realise with a crushing sense of melancholy that for him a world devoid of people would be a much more comfortable place in which to live.

Chapter 51 (233)

Christopher in the shop

The following morning, Mr Shears goes to work, but Christopher's mother takes compassionate leave. She takes him to a shopping centre for clothes and other supplies, but he is frightened by the crowd. He lies on the floor and screams. She takes him home again.

Christopher wants to return to Swindon

He tells her that he has to go back to Swindon, because he has to sit his maths A level. She tries to put off discussion of this. At night, Christopher goes outside and sits hidden between a skip and a van, thinking about tesselated crosses. His mother suddenly appears, terrified at his disappearance. She makes him promise not to leave on his own again. Next morning, his mother hears that she has lost the job. Christopher continues to insist that he has to return to sit the maths exam. His mother is overcome by his demands and her problems. Next day, she takes him to Hampstead Heath (a famous park) and tells him that she has rung and postponed his exam. His reaction?

> Quote
>
> I screamed for a long time and the pain in my chest hurt so much that it was hard to breathe ...

Back at the flat, she has Roger Shears get books for Christopher, but Christopher refuses to read them. She induces Christopher to eat. When she and Mr Shears fight again, Christopher takes the radio and tunes it to the white noise between stations. During the night, Roger Shears, drunk, comes into Christopher's room and yells at him.

The return to Swindon

Next day, Christopher's mother packs and takes him away in Roger's car. Eventually they get back to Swindon. Christopher goes up to his room and plays on the computer. Later, Christopher's father returns. There is a heated exchange between the parents. Christopher groans and bangs on the drums. After an hour, his mother tells him that his father has gone to stay with Rhodri. Again Christopher asks to do the maths exam, but his mother tries to tell him that it has been postponed. She attempts to interest him in science videos and food, but he will not co-operate.

The following day, after a brief (but abusive) encounter with Mrs Shears, she drives him to school. Siobhan tells him that the headmistress still has the A level exam papers, and that they are going to try to get the invigilator to supervise Christopher. She asks him if he wants to sit the exam.

> **Quote**
>
> And I said, 'I want to do it' because I don't like it when I put things in my timetable and I have to take them out again, because when I do that it makes me feel sick.

Christopher sits the maths exam

Christopher sits the first exam. He has to calm himself before he begins.

That night, his father comes back. Christopher screams. Later, he goes to lie in the garden and look at the stars. His father angrily goes away again.

The next day, Christopher does the second exam. That night, Mr Shears arrives, throws the mother's belongings onto the lawn, and drives off in his car.

The following day, Christopher does the last exam. He is pleased with his performance. That night, his father comes to the house again. He asks Christopher how the exam went, and says, **'I'm very proud of you ... I'm sure you did really well'**.

Christopher's mother gets a job and they move into a room together. Christopher waits for the exam results. His mother distracts him with an ingenious puzzle, and with painting the room. But there are many 'bad things'. Sometimes Christopher has to go to his father's house. His father tries to talk to him – **'but I didn't answer him. And sometimes I heard him sitting on the floor outside the door quietly for a long time'**. Also, Toby dies.

The gift of a puppy

One day, Christopher's father asks to talk with him. He begs Christopher to learn to trust him again, no matter how long it takes. Then he tells Christopher that he has a present for him. He gives Christopher a pup. The pup is to remain with the father, and Christopher will visit.

An A grade

Christopher gets his results: an A grade. It makes him feel happy (he signifies this with a smiley face). Christopher calls the pup 'Sandy', and takes him for walks. He stays more often with his father, and helps him with the garden. His father arranges for him to do Further Maths A levels the following year.

Christopher and the future

Christopher visualises the future, in which he will go to university, where he can live in a flat with Sandy, together with his books and his computer. Then he can become a scientist. The text ends:

> Quote
>
> And I know I can do this because I went to London on my own, and because I solved the mystery of Who Killed Wellington? and I found my mother and I was brave and I wrote a book and that means I can do anything.

Commentary

Haddon avoids an overly sentimental denouement in his final chapter. On the one hand, Christopher is back in Swindon, has successfully passed the A level exam, and now has a puppy to cheer him up. On the other hand, the marriage of his parents is still in tatters, and the reconciliation with his father is obviously going to take a long time. There is no escape clause – no cheery Hollywood happy ending. The condition is a cruel one, and whatever 'good things' Haddon allows his central character, there are always going to be plenty of 'bad things' too. The condition is not going to go away, and there can be no miracle cure.

However, the ending *is* upbeat in one respect. Christopher has at least moved on from where he started. His experiences have taught him something. As he reflects on his journey, his 'detecting', his book and the other successes he has carved with such difficulty from the challenges he faced, he realises that 'I can do anything'. It may not be all that accurate a statement (given his very real limitations), but to the extent that understanding and willpower *are* important tools, the author signals reason for hope. Even 'special people' like Christopher can triumph, in small ways, over adversity. The future for him will be a lonely one, but in his own strange way he has the chance to be genuinely happy. The smiley face is apt. Disability is not the end of it. Christopher has won, in so many ways, and 'good things' *are* possible.

Notes on Characters

Christopher John Francis Boone

> I find people confusing. This is for two main reasons. The first reason is that people do a lot of talking without using any words ....The second main reason is that people often talk using metaphors.

Christopher as a complex character – not pathetic but different

Although our first instinct might be to pity Christopher, to think of him as a poor sad individual, this reaction is rather simplistic, and not at all what the author intends. Certainly he has disadvantages, and compared to most people, finds even the everyday rituals of life a challenge. But he is *not* helpless, and he has some very positive qualities, which must be listed alongside his disabilities. It is probably best to resist the urge to put value judgements (particularly 'bad' or 'pathetic') on his ways of doing things, and, along with the author, regard him more as 'different' or 'special'.

Christopher and Aspergers'

The symptoms of Asperger's syndrome have been surveyed in the introductory notes. Christopher himself lists his own selection of them too:

> Not talking to people ... Not eating or drinking ... Not liking being touched ... Screaming when I am angry or confused ... Not liking being in really small places with other people ... Smashing things ... Groaning ... Not liking yellow things or brown things ... Not eating food if different sorts of food are touching each other ... Not noticing that people are angry with me ... Not smiling ... Hitting other people ... (Chapter 21/'73')

The disabilities

This is a serious set of problems, of course. His *emotional* deficit in particular – not relating to feelings and people's non-verbal (body) language – facial expression, tone of voice, etc – puts him at a massive disadvantage. Or consider his aversion to touch – so normal a part of our lives and so huge a consolation for most people. His susceptibility to sensory overload – which he memorably describes at one point as being like a computer 'crashing' – makes him incredibly vulnerable to the world. His literal-mindedness – dealing only in facts and figures, not indulging in imaginative play – deprives him enormously.

The talents and triumphs

Yet to pass Christopher off as just a bundle of twitchy inadequacies is to miss what Haddon is doing with this intriguing character. It is to ignore his very real enthusiasms: his fascination with astronomy, with maths and science, with Sherlock Holmes, with puzzles, with computers. It is to undervalue his perceptiveness and rationality. Think of Chapter 42 ('181'), which starts with the statement 'I see everything'. This is where he explains how he looks at a field full of cows. This is someone who is almost *too* perceptive – his problem is that he misses nothing. Or his astonishing grasp of why things like timetables are meaningful – 'they make sure you don't get lost in time' – which (time) he has just explained at a level involving Einstein's Theory of Relativity. His discussion of why people believe in God, arguing that 'they think it is unlikely that anything as complicated as ... the human eye ... could happen by chance', is effectively university-level philosophy – and he has arrived at such thinking by sheer natural ability. So there are plenty of things to celebrate about Christopher, let us not forget. He is a gifted child, for all his problems.

Negatives

However, he is a sad figure too, to be sure. Haddon does not offer any magic cure. He depicts the condition in all its humdrum misery. Consider for example that awfully sad dream about being in a world devoid of people (after the killer virus) which is in effect a metaphor for Christopher's condition. Or how terrified he is in the Underground at Paddington station, reduced to immobility for five hours by the noise and clamour of trains and people. Or ponder for a moment what we learn about his schoolmates at the 'special needs' school. Think of Joseph who 'plays with it' when he goes to the toilet. Here is a portrait of disability from the inside.

Positives

Yet the novel ends on an upbeat note. Christopher has achieved a lot, has moved forward, and faces the future optimistically. The text is not despairing, despite its often gritty realism. Haddon is really suggesting that individuals like Christopher need sympathy, and help. They are not to be pitied, or despised, but valued.

Ed Boone (Christopher's father)

Quote

I cooked his meals. I cleaned his clothes. I looked after him every weekend. I looked after him when he was ill. I took him to the doctor. I worried myself sick every time he wandered off somewhere at night. I went to school every time he got into a fight ...

The two sides of Ed

Ed is a problematical character. On the one hand he is rough and ready, and in the matter of his monumental lie about the death of Judy, well beyond acceptable behaviour. On the other hand, he clearly cares for the boy, and is deeply unhappy about the falling out. We need to balance our view, acknowledging both sides. Haddon himself defends the father.

Quote

I think that Christopher's father runs counter to the usual stereotype [of the uncaring parent] in that it is he who brings up Christopher on his own. Moreover (and despite the fact that he has huge and obvious failings) many readers think that he does represent a positive influence in Christopher's life, and I have had many letters from parents of young people with Asperger's who recognise a lot of what he has to go through. (*Guardian* interview, cited above)

Another reviewer offers this comment: 'Struggling to bring up his autistic son alone, the father is the most poignant character in the book, for his unconditional love is never reciprocated' (*The Australian*, 2 August 2003). Perhaps one of the most telling comments from Ed is this:

Quote

God knows, I try, Christopher, God knows I do, but ... Life is difficult, you know. It's bloody hard telling the truth all the time.

What Haddon reminds us in his depiction of Ed Boone is that living with a disabled person *is* difficult. No matter how hard a parent or other carer tries, the challenges can sometimes be almost overwhelming.

Ed as a reminder of the problems of carers

How do carers cope? Sometimes well, showing patience and wisdom. Sometimes stupidly, as in Ed's silly (if understandable) lie about Judy, or the rage ('that red mist') which leads to the death of Wellington, or in his clumsy attempts to get Christopher back. But throughout the story, there is no real doubt about the one important element – his love for the boy. The reason the end of the narrative shows us a tentative rapprochement – the gift of the puppy, the gardening and the slow rebuilding of trust – is that Ed cares enough to keep trying, even in the face of rejection and a seemingly impossible task. That is important. Haddon reminds readers that working with a disabled child (or adult for that matter) requires, above all, this extraordinary commitment. All the rest is detail. Without love, nothing is going to work.

Judy Boone (Christopher's mother)

Quote

If you ever do that again, I swear to God, Christopher, I love you, but ... I don't know what I'll do.

Judy disputes the stereotypes

Haddon is an original thinker. The easy, or default, scenario, would have been to show the mother as the saintly carer, who puts up with whatever the disabled person does. Haddon knows, and invites us to see, that it all depends on the personality of the individual. Gender does not predetermine the answer. In this case, the father (Ed) is the more patient one. The mother is more in-clined to lose her temper and give up.

The author is not, however, inviting us to scorn the mother. The worst thing she does is run away with Roger Shears, but even that is explained:

Quote

And it made me so sad because it was like you didn't really need me at all. And somehow that was even worse than you and me arguing all the time because it was like I was invisible.

The letters she writes give a clear enough account of what made living with Christopher hard and, if we forget these, consider the scene in the John Lewis store (Chapter 51/'233') when Judy is just trying to buy clothes for Christopher – he lies on the floor and screams until she takes him home. Like the father, she is no saint, but like him she redeems herself (after a two-year interval). She basically means well, and simply doesn't know what to do. We *feel* for Judy, despite her earlier abandonment of the boy, and see that she was constantly struggling to reconcile her feelings as a mother with her needs as a woman.

The fact that she comes back into Christopher's life is important. Her tolerance of Ed reappearing, talking to the boy, offering him the puppy, is a pointer to her caring attitude. Like Ed, she reminds us that perseverance and love are indispensable in dealing with a disabled family member.

Siobhan (Christopher's teacher)

Quote

You don't have to do [the exam], Christopher. If you say you don't want to do it no one is going to be angry with you .... It will just be what you want and that will be fine.

A number of people in the world outside Christopher's immediate family appear in the book. These range from highly sympathetic characters like Siobhan and Mrs Alexander through to rather off-hand individuals like the policeman, and even downright unpleasant ones like Roger Shears.

Siobhan the ideal carer?

Siobhan can perhaps be taken as an idealised, but believable, portrait of the institutional carer. As Christopher's main teacher at the special school, she employs methods which display sound training and quite a bit of intuitive understanding. She is compassionate and flexible. She sees that urging him to face challenges, and improve himself, is important, but that it is a delicate process, and that if she pushes too hard, he can be easily daunted. Her dealing with the maths exam (as above) is masterly – coaxing but accepting of any possible response on his part. This gentle approach pays off handsomely, as his success and enhanced self-concept show.

Siobhan is the face we would want to see in all teachers, all carers – smart, sensitive, non-judgemental – the sort of person who can get the most out of any individual, no matter what their problems.

Notes on Themes and Issues

Mental disabilities and the need for understanding

> But Siobhan said we have to use [the term 'Special Needs'] because people used to call children like the children at school *spaz* and *crip* and *mong* which were nasty words. But that is stupid too because sometimes the children from the school down the road see us in the street when we're getting off the bus and they shout, 'Special Needs! Special Needs!'

Mental problems are not a rarity. They are extremely common. The question is not 'Should something be done about the disabled?' but '*How* are the disabled to be treated?' The passage above provides a quick reminder of unsatisfactory responses. The book as a whole provides a guide to more appropriate ones.

The novel engages the whole mental health debate

It is worth noting immediately that Haddon does not pretend that dealing with the disabled is easy. Apart from trying to find ways to help them, so far as that is possible, there is the everyday difficulty of simply living with them. When Christopher's mother finds herself at the end of her tether, which is quite often, we are forced to recall that even family are very taxed in the face of such challenges, let alone strangers.

To ignore the plight of the disabled is not a proper stance. The whole text is implicitly an argument for care and understanding. But *what* is the best approach? *The Curious Incident* effectively deals with several issues within this debate.

The 'deficit' model?

Should we treat them as mentally crippled, and not expect anything much from them? This deficit or determinist (and defeatist) mentality, caricatured perhaps in the jeers of the children from other schools, and even seen fleetingly in the attitude of Judy Boone – for whom the maths exam is almost an irrelevance (because what does it really matter?) is *not* acceptable, Haddon implies. How do we know? Because he makes quite a strong case for Christopher's abilities, and his *need* to be extended. The triumph Christopher experiences when he gets an 'A' for the Year 12 maths exam (at the age of 15) is a major clue here. To have treated Christopher as a basket case who will never amount to anything is a long way from his own (Christopher's) view of himself, and fundamentally unfair. The cry of 'I can do anything' with which the text ends is no accident. It is a rebuttal of the 'spaz' and 'crip' perception.

The differences are illusory model?

Should we then see them as just like everyone else – declare their differences an illusion (a prejudice) and adopt what could be caricatured as a 'they're really quite normal – just misunderstood' view? In welfare circles there has been a tendency to see 'deficit' thinking as politically incorrect and to easily make the logical slide to thinking there must be ways to 'fix' the problems – and to imply that if we *don't* (fix the disabled), we're just not trying hard enough. This too is critiqued by the author. If, following him on his adventures through the narrative, we had begun to think that Christopher is really quite 'normal', for all his quirks, the John Lewis (shop) scene may be there to startle us out of our complacency. Haddon worked with the disabled, and he implicitly argues that people like Christopher will *always* be different. It is not just a matter of semantics. A disabled person is *really* disabled.

The fostering and enhancing model

The text seems to imply that the best strategy is one that enhances and fosters the potential of the disabled. Like the character Siobhan, who clear-sightedly acknowledges Christopher's problems, and then finds ways of building on them – the 'how to read faces' strategy, the writing journal, the exam – trying to add value to the life of a disabled person is a sound strategy. The same idea is built into Ed Boone's attempts at reconciliation. His device of the puppy, his offer of gardening as a therapy, are examples of little steps keyed into the disabled person's needs and interests. He doesn't give up (the 'spaz' argument). He doesn't assume all's well (the 'normal' argument). He starts with where Christopher is, and builds on that.

A related issue, which is at the heart of the novel, is: What is mental disability like? How does it feel to be disabled? Have such people anything in common with 'normal' people?

Quote

No one is ever really a stranger. We cling to the belief that we share nothing with certain people. It's rubbish. We have almost everything in common with everyone. (*Guardian* interview, cited above)

He sees Christopher not as 'ill', but certainly as 'different'. The novel is a plea for understanding. Most people either suffer from mental distress at some time in their lives, or have contact with someone who is distressed or disabled.

> We want to think we're different from disabled people to protect our normality, but Christopher's plight is universal because we all love order, pattern, ritual. It gives comfort, but we don't notice unless someone breaks the rules. (*Sunday Times*, 1 February 2004)

Haddon did not want the terms 'autism' or 'Asperger's syndrome' to be put on the book's cover. He was overridden by the publisher, in fact, but his wish is revealing. Here are two other comments that he has made on the subject:

> 'The label [Asperger's syndrome] doesn't add anything to our knowledge of anyone,' says the author, who would prefer it if the term 'odd' were to become popular again. 'In the old days you were allowed to be odd,' he says. 'Too many people now who would have been odd find themselves with a label and getting sucked into some kind of system …. [It's important to remember that] people with Asperger's are as varied as Norwegians or trombone players.' He's already heard from parents thanking him for his humanising portrait of autism. (*Newsweek*, 8 September 2003)

Christopher: an argument for understanding and respect

One of the text's most poignant aspects is that Christopher doesn't feel there's something *odd* about him: he sees *his* way of looking at the world as normal, even superior (as his comments on God suggest). It's everyone else, in a sense, who has the problem. For him, the number obsessions, the fear of strangers and touching and the mystery of emotions are in their way quite reasonable. If we look at how Haddon positions us to regard his central character, we would have to say that Christopher is *not* depicted as a freak. He is a real person, with needs, vulnerabilities' and aspirations and he has a legitimate call on our respect.

Dysfunctional families

> I used to think Mother and Father might get divorced. That was because they had lots of arguments and sometimes they hated each other. This is because of the stress of looking after someone who has Behavioural Problems like I have.

If we ask why Wellington (the dog in the night-time) was killed, the answer is Ed Boone's anger at being abandoned by Judy and then, after a transitory affair, by Mrs Shears. In short, the dog died because of the grown ups' chaotic emotional life. So in a sense the emblematic dog (of the title) points to the issue of dysfunctional families.

Causes of family breakdown

What can go wrong in families? Clearly falling out of love, growing bored, indulging in adultery, separating or divorcing are common problems. The Boone family are an example, as are the Shears. All involved tend to suffer – not just the feuding parents, but the children (or pets) caught in the crossfire. In a sense, Wellington is just another casualty of the mess.

A further reason for family breakdown, and this is underlined subtly in the novel, is abnormal pressure, or major stressors. It may come from a range of factors – economic, social, psychological – from *outside* or from *within*. There is economic hardship (poverty, unemployment), social disadvantage (the problems of racial or socially induced hardship) and mental problems – whether caused by genetic reasons (most mental illness has strong genetic components), drug taking, or accident. *The Curious Incident* deals with a family which struggles to cope with an autistic child. This child is afflicted by the relatively milder ('high functioning') condition, Asperger's. But it is still enough to make life unbearable for the more highly strung Judy Boone.

Families and the disabled

> I am just about holding this together. But I am this close to losing it, all right?

We are invited to imagine what it would be like to find one's child lying on the floor and screaming in a department store, or having to coax him to accept red (only) drinks using a points system of rewards, or simply missing out on ever touching him.

The strain has broken up the Boone family, and although the ending of the text suggests a tentative truce, the marriage is over and life with Christopher remains a kind of endurance test.

A hard look at families

What Haddon reminds us is that family life – normally an iconic thing (as sacred for most people as motherhood) – can in fact be a crucible of difficulties, a battlefield. Whether because of the weakness of the individuals – and the Boones are *very* fallible people, as Ed's outbursts and Judy's letters make clear – or the abnormal pressures placed on the family, relationships can break down quite easily. And the consequences are hard on everyone involved. Haddon has suggested that he wanted to expose this reality.

> Quote
>
> Children's fiction is [normally surrounded by] a little invisible ring of safety. I wanted to say, 'This is the real world. Bad things might happen.' (*Sunday Times* interview, cited above)

Coping with life ... the challenge of experience and emotion

> Quote
>
> I think there's a part in all of us that would really like to be Christopher for a few days. Taking other people into account is such hard work. (Mark Haddon, *Newsweek*, cited above)

A 'coming of age' novel?

Although it may seem a curious thing to suggest, at one level *The Curious Incident* can be read as a 'coming of age' or 'growing up' narrative. Consider this passage (from 43/'191'):

> Quote
>
> And it was like standing on a cliff in a really strong wind because it made me feel giddy and sick and because there were lots of people walking into and out of the tunnel and it was really echoey ... So I said to myself ... 'I will walk down the tunnel ...' and I walked down the tunnel trying to concentrate on the sign at the end of the tunnel ... And it was like stepping off the cliff on to a tightrope.

Repeatedly, in the latter part of the novel, Christopher almost crumples under the stress of what he has to do, as he moves out of his comfort zone, grapples with terrifying new experiences, and tries to tolerate the fear in order to achieve goals he has set himself.

For most young people, walking down the tunnel (pedestrian underpass) of a railway station is no great challenge. But plenty of other typical adolescent experiences *do* provoke a similar kind of panic: school, the opposite sex, exams, public speaking, job interviews – the list goes on. We all instinctively recognise Christopher's fear of the unknown. His terror may be unusual, in that, because of his condition, it is associated with things we consider ordinary and unthreatening. But we *still* understand the fear. Equally however, we see that he must confront this fear and overcome it if he is to make any headway.

Christopher as an example of all adolescents

And this is the point of connection. Christopher's experiences approximate the universal paradigm of growing up: the gradual facing of challenges, the mastery of new experiences, the growing confidence, the emergence into a type of independence. Even Christopher's 'break' with his parents – first his father, then his mother – is itself paradigmatic. All adolescents must gradually disconnect themselves from their parents in order to stand on their own and face the world as individuals in their own right.

It is not just independence (making your own decisions, facing fears unaided) which is a problem. The very experience of grappling with the world can be a frightening thing – for the world *is* dauntingly complex and vast. No matter how much we try to control our lives, and our dealings with others, the sheer size of the undertaking is formidable. Consider this revealing passage from the novel:

> Quote
>
> And then the countryside started and there were fields and cows and horses and a bridge and a farm and more houses and lots of little roads with cars on. And that made me think that there must be millions of miles of train track in the world and they all go past houses and roads and rivers and fields, and that made me think how many people must be in the world and they all have houses and roads to travel on and pets and clothes and they all eat lunch and go to bed and have names and this made my head hurt ... so I closed my eyes again and did counting and groaning.

Facing the world

What Christopher is troubled by here is the very unknowability of the world. It is too big, too disparate, to grasp. We are, necessarily, able to understand and control only a tiny proportion of our existence. Haddon remarked in one interview:

> Quote

> All of us feel, to a certain extent, alienated from the stuff going on around us. And all of us at some point, rather like Christopher, have chaos entering our lives. We have these limited strategies we desperately use to try to put our lives back in order. So although in some senses he's a very odd and alien character, his situation is not that far removed from situations we've all been in at one time or another. (Interview in powells.com)

Even worse than the world itself, in the sense of the myriad sensory data that bombards us (sights, sounds, smells, sensations of all kinds), is that particularly human kind of input which is

Facing people and feelings

especially difficult for someone like Christopher: *feelings*. In the course of the story, he learns first that his father has committed what amount to crimes (killed, lied, falsified the death of Judy) and then that his mother, whom he thought dead, is simply living with a man not her husband in London. The confession of Ed (39/ '167') is a significant turning point. The emotional torrent that overwhelms Christopher at this point reduces him to a virtually catatonic state. Like the computer overload metaphor, he simply shuts down for a while, unable to cope.

Throughout the novel, emotions are the most challenging problems of all for Christopher. Now he is especially disadvantaged in this sphere. However, beyond the drama of Christopher's crises involving feeling, or interaction with other people, we glimpse a more general idea – that dealing with people and feelings *is* difficult. When Siobhan draws faces for Christopher as a cue to reading people, we feel sad, because we instinctively know that you need to be much subtler than that, much faster in 'reading' human interaction, than a set of pictures could enable you to be. Yet, no matter how 'normal', you may always find keeping up with people's changing feelings, and needs, and weaknesses, and unpredictabilities, a challenge. To this extent, in an exaggerated but very revealing way, Christopher is a sort of case study in the problem of dealing with people – the biggest life challenge of all.

How does Christopher cope? By finding strategies which calm him (like the mental maths, putting his problems in perspective) and by working out solutions. Fortunately, his major strength is to have a logical mind, to see the point of thinking itself. Unlike many people, who just float through life on their emotions, Christopher thinks about what is happening, and tries to find sensible options. Sometimes these are quite literally alternatives which he carefully eliminates. Sometimes they are mental pathways. Here he is at Paddington Station, trying to find his way out:

Coping mechanisms

> So I stood up and I imagined that there was a big red line on the ground which ran parallel to the train to the gate at the far end and I walked along it and I said 'Left, right, left, right ...' again, like before.

By these sorts of devices, he gradually finds his way, not just off the station, but through the challenges of his life.

The importance of communication

> Once I didn't talk to anyone for 5 weeks. (Footnote to Christopher's first point under his list of 'Behavioural Problems', 21/73)

The text as symbolic

Siobhan urges Christopher to 'write something I would want to read myself' as a form of therapy. The text itself therefore becomes a reaching out from an autistic child to other people. Haddon is obviously very focussed on communication. He has said:

> Obviously, on some level [it's about disability], but on another level … it's a book about books, about what you can do with words and what it means to communicate with someone in a book. Here's a character whom if you met him in real life you'd never, ever get inside his head. Yet something magical happens when you write a novel about him. You slip inside his head, and it seems like the most natural thing in the world. (powells.com)

What Haddon achieves by this remarkable novel is letting us inside the world of a disabled individual. It is impossible to finish the novel without a better understanding of, and sympathy for, people like Christopher.

Quote

I never thought a novel about a boy with Asperger's living in Swindon would sell. But at the heart of all my favourite novels is that [same] quality of empathy − E.M. Forster's [famous dictum] 'only connect'. Ultimately, no one is that different from anyone else. (*Sunday Times* interview)

The novel argues for words as a solution

Communication is more than just a tool for the author, a vehicle for a worthy theme. It is an *argument* in its own right. Haddon suggests that listening, talking, reading and writing are the *key* to a better life. Consider the gap between Christopher and his father after Ed is exposed in his lie and the 'murder' he committed. Christopher will not even tolerate him in the same room, for a time. How is this impasse resolved? With *words*.

It takes some time but the father's words, the reaching out to his traumatised child, eventually pay off. The novel ends with a kind of rapprochement. Christopher may be a little wary, but he has moved back into what approximates a trusting, nurturing relationship. Interestingly, this is transacted not in embraces or tears − but in *words*. The focus is revealing.

Communication − literally making meaningful connection with another person − is one of the author's major points. Look, he seems to say, words can help you understand a disabled person. Words can mend wounds. Words are powerful. Sometimes they are used in discordant ways − think of the various outbursts in the novel from angry people (Ed, Judy, Roger, Mrs Shears, assorted uncomprehending strangers) − but ultimately they are a key element in fostering understanding. The alternative, depicted in its extreme (pathological) form in Christopher's non-communication, is linked to maladjustment. Words are not the solution to all problems, but the author implies that they go a long way to building bridges, and making life more tolerable for everyone.

What the Critics Say

The Curious Incident is a masterpiece. Simple as that. (Tim Pigot, *Sunday Territorian*, 7 March 2004)

[Christopher is] a kind of Holden Caulfield [central character in the famous *The Catcher in the Rye*] who speaks bravely and winningly from inside the sorrow of autism: wonderful, simple, easy, moving and likely to be a smash [hit]. (*Kirkus Reviews*, 15 April 2003)

Haddon deftly expressed Christopher's mind games, spinning a story with quiet but powerful irony. (*Library Journal*, Vol. 129, 2003)

Certainly this is an affecting book, an intriguing book, a loving book. (*Times*, 28 January 2004)

Haddon's skill in fusing depth, humour and truth into a difficult subject is remarkable. His lengthy apprenticeship in children's writing – he has written 15 books – has given him a sound base for characterisation and an elegant simplicity of language. Christopher's journey to London – recalling Huckleberry Finn's journey along the Mississippi – evokes observations into human behaviour that are microcosm, however cruel, of Western society. Like *The Adventures of Huckleberry Finn*, this book [will] appear on school reading lists in years to come. (*The Australian*, cited above)

Mark Haddon's stark, funny and original first novel … is presented as a detective story. But it eschews [avoids] most of the furnishings of high-literary enterprise as well as the conventions of genre, disorienting and reorienting the reader to devastating effect. (*New York Times Sunday Book Review*, 2003)

Mark Haddon's portrayal of an emotionally dissociated mind is a superb achievement. He is a wise and bleakly funny writer with rare gifts of empathy. (Ian McEwan, Booker Prize winner and celebrated English author)

Sample Essays

Part 1 Essay

'At the beginning of the novel, we think that the mystery of the dead dog is central to the story. By the end, we know that the real mystery is Christopher Boone himself – his problems in trying to cope with life, but also his amazing capacity to transcend his disability.'

Discuss.

Topic engaged directly, and explicated briefly

The Curious Incident of the Dog in the Night-time starts with a moment of high drama. It is just before midnight. Wellington the dog is dead, a garden fork stuck through his side. Christopher Boone, the first person on the scene, is a lover of Sherlock Holmes and amateur sleuth, so he is soon on the case, sifting through the clues, trying to find out who killed Wellington. Who can resist a murder mystery? We are drawn in immediately, eager, with Christopher, to track down the culprit. Yet the case of the dead dog is soon overshadowed by a bigger problem: who is *Christopher*, and what is wrong with him? The first clue to that is his number for 'Chapter 1': 2. The second clue is his next chapter (called by him number 3). In this, we meet, via his recollection of Siobhan's face cue sheets, someone who can't even read the facial expression 'sad'. Shortly after, Mrs Shears (the dog's owner) starts screaming; a policeman arrives, grabs Christopher, and gets

Both dimensions dealt with in turn

punched for his trouble – and Christopher ends up in custody. And what does he think about on the way to jail? The Milky Way! It hasn't taken long for a 'murder mystery novel' (Christopher's description of the text) to morph into something completely different – a first person narrative about mental disability.

Discussion of the first "mystery" element

There is a very shrewd method in Mark Haddon's strategy. Had he revealed his subtext too blatantly – announcing at the outset that this would be a text exposing the tragedy of mental problems – most readers would doubtless have closed the book. An author has every right to take the didactic approach on a subject like this, effectively waving a banner labelled 'Greater understanding for the mentally challenged'. But such an approach is likely to leave only a committed few to hear his message. What Haddon actually *does*, in *The Curious Incident of the Dog in the Night-time,* is astonishingly clever. The message is itself a mystery. Because the novel has levels. On the surface is a 'murder mystery' – the one about the dog, which Christopher thinks he's writing for his teacher, Siobhan. Beneath this is the mystery of what ails *Christopher* – his autism. And beneath *this* is the author's *real* point – which we only grasp far into an engrossing story, driven along by our fascination with the dead dog case, and by Christopher's calamitous life experiences – that people like Christopher (and their carers) deserve special sympathy, for they are living with almost impossible burdens, and still managing a kind of heroism. The strategy pays off. The novel is not a 'bleeding heart' mental health pamphlet. It is an inspiring human drama.

Story elements appear only as part of the essay's argument

If we look at the 'mystery' of Christopher Boone, we can fairly readily identify his problem. He has Asperger's syndrome or high-functioning autism. That's why Siobhan drew the faces, so he could make some sort of guess at what people were thinking. As Christopher explains, 'I find people confusing'. Essentially Christopher lives in his own world, detached even from his mother and father, who cannot touch him, and can only struggle to understand how he makes sense of things. Christopher has 'Good Days' and 'Bad Days'. The latter tend to involve changed routines, unfamiliar places, too much stimulation. When the world overwhelms Christopher, he explains, 'I make this noise [groaning] when there is too much information coming into my head from the outside world'. His symptoms may be classic Asperger's, but this is not the whole story.

Discussion of the second mystery element: Christopher

Our early impressions of Christopher, as we find out he has no friends, screams when he is confused, groans to shut out stimuli, and acts like what schoolchildren call 'spazzers', may tend to suggest he is a hopeless case. But part of the mystery which Haddon explores is his resilience, his will to survive, even triumph. What is particularly clever about the mystery motif is that the levels of the novel connect so well. Christopher's murder investigation leads, accidentally, to uncovering the truth about his mother and father (another mystery). It is a truth that is initially quite traumatic. Christopher has what amounts to a breakdown: 'It was like someone had switched me off and then switched me on again'. Yet beyond the trauma lies a challenge – the need he suddenly

The topic's 'mystery' concept explored in sophisticated ways

experiences to find his mother – to get out of what he suddenly sees as an intolerable situation. That in turn leads to the epic journey to London, and to his being reunited with Judy Boone. Christopher never becomes 'normal'. He has a fit when his mother takes him shopping. He still refuses to touch either parent, or to fully trust his father. But for all that, he has made real progress. That is why the novel ends with these rapturous words: 'I went to London on my own, and ... I solved the mystery of Who Killed Wellington? and I found my mother and I was brave and I wrote a book and that means I can do anything'.

The solving of the dog's murder is ultimately a trivial matter. In the larger scheme of the text, it is little more than a narrative ploy to get us involved. What it leads Christopher to, and readers, is far more significant. First there is the exposure, as *Conclusion* Christopher tells his story, of *Christopher himself* – a portrait at *returns to* once naïve (because he misses so many things) and sophisti-*the topic* cated (because the author allows us to read between the lines and *overall, and* see what is really happening). Here we have a powerful recreation *'wraps up'* of what it's like to be autistic. Even there, the author is at pains to *eloquently* show that it's not all 'Black Days'. Christopher is clever, and eager to make the most of the hand fate has dealt him. As he reacts to the truths and traumas of his life, he makes a journey of discovery and conquest – of himself. And that he can actually make such stunning progress is another part of the mystery. Finally, there is more than just bad news in this story of disability. There is hope as well. We end the novel not with a sense of having been lectured or browbeaten, but with a sense of privilege at being able to live for a while inside the mind of a person like Christopher.

Part 2 Essay

'*The Curious Incident of the Dog in the Night-time* tells us that we have more things in common with others, even with the mentally disabled, than we have differences.'

Do you agree?

In the interests of honesty, Christopher at one point lists his 'Behavioural Problems'. They include 'Not talking to people ...

Not eating or drinking anything for a long time ... Not liking being touched ... Screaming when I am angry or confused ... Smashing things ... Groaning ... Not liking yellow things or brown things ... Not smiling ... Hitting people ...'. The list gives us what amount to casebook Asperger's symptoms – the outward signs of someone locked up in a private world, emotionally retarded, seriously disabled. Yet to focus on the disabilities of the central character is to miss a larger truth in *The Curious Incident of the Dog in the Night-time*. Christopher, for all his weird behaviour and problems, is a very sympathetic character. We finish the novel not shunning

him but embracing him. He may live life in a strange, and deeply challenging, way – but we recognise a great deal about him that is like us. The connection between the disabled and the rest of us is a major part of the novel's subtext.

On the face of it, Christopher is an alien consciousness. If he sees a series of yellow cars in the street, it is a Black Day. Why? Because yellow is a 'bad' colour. If different kinds of food are

touching on his plate, he can't eat it. If a person smiles at him, he struggles to guess at what it could mean. If someone tries to touch him, he freaks out. If he looks into a field, he sees every tiny detail in it, and risks mental collapse. Even Christopher recognises that he goes to a Special School, full of disabled pupils: 'All the children at my school are stupid,' he says bluntly at one stage. When he accidentally comes upon a letter from his 'dead' mother, all he can say is 'Lots of things are mysteries' – and distract himself by calculating the frog population in a pond. Some days later, when the truth dawns on him, after two whole years, that his mother is alive and living in London, he vomits and suffers a sort of breakdown. The journey that he then undertakes, with pet rat Toby his only companion, is a nightmare ordeal. Why? Because it means finding the station, buying a ticket, reading the Underground map, tolerating the big city crowds – what are mere colourful details to the rest of the world. Christopher is disabled, and we rarely forget it.

Yet for all his differences, he is also very like everyone else, in certain ways. The novel starts with him finding the dead dog, Wellington, and deciding to solve the mystery. He is arrested when he hits a policeman, and on his way to the police station looks up at the stars – distracting himself from the trouble he is in. The policeman offers him the chance to lie about his motives, and get off. Christopher has to struggle with this oldest of ethical dilemmas, as most people would. When he finds out that his mother has run away and his father has lied to him, he is horrified. The strength of his reaction is extreme, but every reader can understand why he is traumatised. He is like any other child growing up the hard way, and discovering bit by bit that the world is a careless and cruel place. Even his mental obsessions, like maths and science, take on the shape of a coping strategy. They are orderly systems to set against the chaos of real life. As he says at one stage, '... Maths wasn't like life because in life there are no straightforward answers at the end'. Even the traumas of his rail trip to London, while far beyond the normal, contain echoes of everyone's fear of the unknown. How many foreign travellers have found themselves in some noisy, threatening place, where nothing makes sense – and felt the panic rising in them, not all that different in tone from Christopher's? When his father tries to explain the whole sorry saga to him – 'that red mist [came] down ... everything I'd been bottling up for years just [came out] ...we're not that different, you and me' – Christopher feels conflicted (to trust or not to trust) just like *any* child who has been betrayed. And when he starts to get better, with the triumphant maths A level exam, and the gift of the puppy, he is exactly like anyone else who begins to heal again after a trauma.

Detailed use of example, quote, integration of story and topic

Mark Haddon does not really seek to underplay the difficulties of the disabled. 'I couldn't take it anymore,' says Judy in one of her letters, trying to explain why she left home, abandoning her child. Ed is even more direct: 'Christopher, if you do not behave I swear I will knock the living daylights out of you'. When Judy takes Christopher to the store to buy pyjamas, he falls onto the floor and screams, until she takes him home. This is *after* the journey to London, in case we think him 'cured'. To the extent that the novel invites us to think about the problems of disability in the wider community, we are not urged to think such problems illusory. Statistics tell us that 2.5% of the population have serious psychiatric disabilities, and that mental illness – including conditions such as depression, anxiety, and so on – may afflict up to 20% of the community at any one time. People who cannot function properly because of autism, or dementia, or brain damage, are in need of real help. Their similarities to ordinary folk – that is their humanity and their rights to be treated well – can never obscure the fact that their differences are real, and need special attention. Haddon does *not* imply that Christopher is perfectly normal, and

Extrapolation of the topic to the broader themes involved (Part 2)

that his future will be trouble-free. He still lives in a strange, lonely place, and for all the ending's upbeat tone, we know that life will never, for him, be easy.

However, the novel *is* about communicating and sharing experiences. We are as inclined to laugh with Christopher, and to find ourselves thinking about the curious wisdom of what he says, as we are to cry for him, let alone reject him. His startling insights, like 'People believe in God because the world is very complicated and they think it ... unlikely that anything as complicated as a flying squirrel or ... a brain could happen by chance' and even his view on holidays – a waste of time because 'a thing is interesting because of thinking about it and not because of it being new' – force us to enter his world, and share his views, if only for a time. We find ourselves having a common experience of people, and life, and this counts finally far more than the differences.

Conclusion balances both aspects of the topic – and sums up neatly

Sample Questions

Part 1 Questions

1 'Although traumatic, Christopher's challenges help him break out of his mental prison.'

Discuss.

2 'Haddon's greatest achievement is to make the inner world of a mentally disabled individual real to us, and to invite our deepest sympathy.'

How does he achieve this?

3 'We may abhor, even despise, Christopher's parents, but we are certainly able to understand their difficulties in dealing with his "Behavioural Problems".'

Discuss.

Part 2 Questions

4 '*The Curious Incident of the Dog in the Night-time* is a dramatic plea for understanding those with mental disabilities.'

Discuss.

5 '*The Curious Incident of the Dog in the Night-time* seems to be a portrait of despair, but it finally ends up a novel with a message of hope.'

Do you agree?

6 '*The Curious Incident of the Dog in the Night-time* demonstrates how challenging life is, not just for the disabled, but for everyone.'

Discuss.

Titles in this series so far

The Accidental Tourist
Angela's Ashes
Antigone
Away
Border Crossing
Brave New World / Blade Runner
Breaker Morant
Briar Rose
Brilliant Lies
The Brush-Off
Cabaret
Cat's Eye
The Chant of Jimmie Blacksmith
Cloudstreet
The Collector
Cosi
The Crucible
The Curious Incident of the dog in the
    night-time
The Divine Wind
Dispossessed
Diving for Pearls
Educating Rita
Emma & Clueless
Falling
Fly Away Peter
Follow Your Heart
The Freedom of the City
Frontline
Gattaca
Girl with a Pearl Earring
Going Home
A Good Scent from a Strange Mountain
Great Expectations
The Great Gatsby
Hamlet
The Handmaid's Tale
Hard Times
Henry Lawson's Stories
I for Isobel
An Imaginary Life
I'm not scared
In Between
In Country
In the Lake of the Woods
The Inheritors
The Journey Area of Study
King Lear
The Kitchen God's Wife
Lantana
A Lesson before Dying

Letters from the Inside
The Life and Crimes of Harry Lavender
Lives of Girls and Women
Lionheart
The Longest Memory
Looking for Alibrandi
The Lost Salt Gift of Blood
Macbeth
Maestro
A Man for All Seasons
Medea
Montana 1948
My Left Foot
My Name is Asher Lev
My Place
Night
Nineteen Eighty-Four
No Great Mischief
Oedipus Rex
Of Love and Shadows
One True Thing
Othello
The Outsider
Paper Nautilus
The Plague
The Player
Pride and Prejudice
The Quiet American
Rabbit-Proof Fence
Raw
Remembering Babylon
The Riders
Schindler's List
Scission
Shakespeare in Love
The Shipping News
Sometimes Gladness
Stolen
Strictly Ballroom
Things Fall Apart
Tirra Lirra by the River
Travels with my Aunt
The Truman Show
A View from the Bridge
We All Fall Down
What's Eating Gilbert Grape
The Wife of Martin Guerre
Wild Cat Falling
Witness
Wrack